WOHLFAHRT

60 STUDIES

Opus 45

VOLUME II

FOR VIOLA

(JOSEPH VIELAND)

Published in 2019 by Allegro Editions

60 Studies for Viola (Book 2)
ISBN: 978-1-9748-9975-3 (paperback)

Cover design by Kaitlyn Whitaker

Cover image: "*Viola*" by r. ufuk vural courtesy of Shutterstock;
"*Music Sheet*" by danielo courtesy of Shutterstock

ALLEGRO
EDITIONS

60 STUDIES
Opus 45
VOLUME II

Edited by *JOSEPH VIELAND*

FRANZ WOHLFAHRT
(1833-1884)

Nº 31. Moderato.

VIOLA

№ 32. Allegro.

4

Allegro Moderato.

Nº 34. Allegro.

6

N⁰ 35. Allegro.

Nº 36. Moderato.

Nº 37. Moderato.

8

Nº 38. Moderato.

№ 39. Moderato.

10

Nº 40. Allegro scherzando.

N⁰ 41. Allegro Moderato.

12

No 42. Andante.

No 43. Moderato.

13

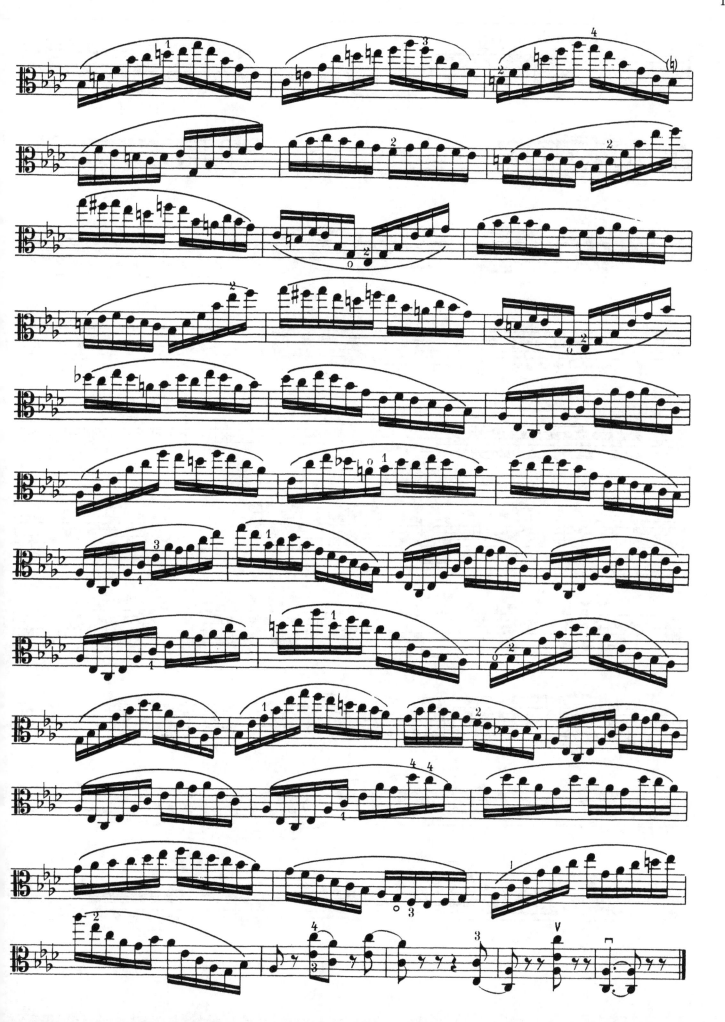

Nº 44. Tempo di Marcia.

Nº 45. Moderato.

Nº 46. Allegro.

Nº 47. Andante cantabile.

18

Nº 50. Allegro.

N° 51. Moderato.

№ 52. Andante.

№ 53. Andante.

cre - scen - - do

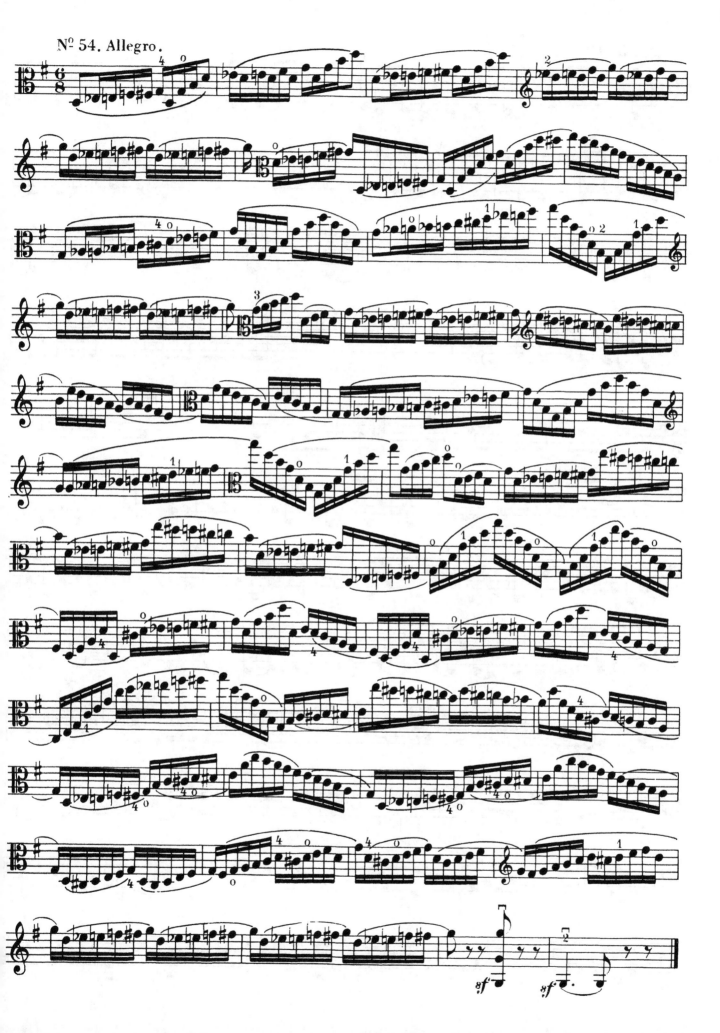

Nº 55. Allegro.

26

Nº 57. Moderato assai.

Nº 58. Andante.

N.° 59. Moderato assai.

Nº 60. Allegro con fuoco.